Old BANGOR

by
John Hanna

The view of Main Street from its intersection with Hamilton Road and Castle Street. In order to ge... ...aph must have been taken from the roof of what was originally Bangor's Market House. The steeple of th... ...gor Presbyterian Church dominates the view. The church was built in 1837 and the steeple added in 1881. The signs for Van Houten's Cocoa are at Warden's Corner which was named after the shop with all the goods on the pavement. The railings to the right belonged to the Town Hall, formerly Bangor Endowed School, which was built in 1856. This was demolished in the 1930s.

Text © John Hanna, 2003.
First published in the United Kingdom, 2003,
by Stenlake Publishing Limited,
01290 551122
www.stenlake.co.uk
ISBN 9781840332414

Printed by
Berforts, 17 Burgess Road, Hastings, TN35 4NR

The publishers regret that they cannot supply
copies of any pictures featured in this book.

ACKNOWLEDGEMENTS
The publishers wish to thank Des Quail for permission to reproduce the photographs on the front
cover, the inside front cover and pages 1, 2, 5–7, 12–14, 16–18, 25, 26, 29, 32, 33, 35, 36, 37 (both),
38 (both), 39–42, 44, 45 and 48.

FURTHER READING
The books listed below were used by the author
during his research. None of them are available from
Stenlake Publishing. Those interested in finding out
more are advised to contact their local bookshop or
reference library.

James Nixon, *Royal Ulster – A Yacht Club and its
House*, Royal Ulster Yacht Club, 1999.

Marcus Patton, *Bangor – An Historical Gazetteer*,
Ulster Architectural Heritage Society, 1999.

Ian Wilson, *North Down – A Century of Photographs*,
North Down Heritage Centre, 1999.

Ian Wilson and Andrew Jaggers, *Bangor Bay and
Harbour – A Pictorial History*, North Down
Heritage Centre, 2002.

This postcard, sent in 1904, shows HMS *Exmouth* in Bangor Bay. A battleship of the Duncan Class, *Exmouth* was launched on 31 August 1901, and had a displacement tonnage of 14,000 tons and a speed of 19 knots. Manned by 750 sailors, its main armaments were four 12 inch guns and the ship also had four torpedo tubes. It became the flagship of the Channel Fleet in 1906 and by July 1912 had become the flagship of the Vice-Admiral while serving with the 4th Battle Squadron in the Home Fleet. In 1915 the ship saw action off the Dardanelles, before returning home in 1917 when it was paid off and went into reserve. It was sold for breaking up in February 1920.

INTRODUCTION

Bangor may take its name from the Gaelic *Beannchar*, which is derived from the Old Norse for 'horned bay'. The first settlements in the area go back to Neolithic times, but it was the founding of the monastery by Saint Comgall in AD 558, and the establishment of a centre of learning, which laid the town's foundation. From the abbey missionaries set out all over Europe to establish links with Bangor and although attacks by marauding Vikings in the ninth century destroyed the abbey, it was restored by Saint Malachy in the twelfth century. The importance of Bangor during those early times is shown by the fact that it was one of only four places in Ireland included in the world map of 1300, the 'Mappa Mundi', which is now on display in Hereford Cathedral.

In the 1500s the abbey once again became a ruin as Henry VIII carried out the Dissolution of the Monasteries. A church replaced it, but this itself was burned down in 1572 during fighting between the O'Neills and English troops.

At the start of the seventeenth century a Scot, Sir James Hamilton, was rewarded with lands around Bangor by King James I. He rebuilt the church and encouraged other Scots to settle in the area. Early Bangor owes a lot to Hamilton who later became Viscount Clandeboye. In 1612 King James made Bangor a borough, entitling it to elect two MPs to the Irish parliament in Dublin. By 1625 there were two principal streets, the present lower Main Street and High Street, which were linked by shoreline development. The Custom House and watchtower built in 1637 are still standing. Hamilton died in 1644 and by 1670 he had no direct descendants.

The lands passed eventually to Anne Hamilton (no relation to Sir James), who in 1710 married Michael Ward of Castle Ward, Strangford. The Wards became the second family to control Bangor and they built the first pier in 1757. It was around this port area that cotton mills were built in the latter part of the eighteenth century, encouraged by Colonel Robert Ward.

The Ward family continued its control of Bangor, even after the passing of the Town Improvement Act of 1854. In 1864 the first Town Commissioners were elected and Robert Ward was their first Chairman. The arrival of the Belfast, Holywood and Bangor Railway line in 1865 led to the growth of Bangor, making it accessible as a resort and also as a place from which to commute to Belfast. This led to the development of many fine houses close to the station.

Towards the end of the nineteenth century efforts were being made to improve the town as a tourist resort. The remains of the mills were removed from the seafront and an esplanade was created at the bottom of Ballymagee Street, complete with a bandstand. In 1905 further access for the public was provided with the acquisition, by an Act of Parliament, of the seafront road around to Strickland's Glen and soon Ballyholme Park, Ward Park and Strickland's Glen became public places.

By the end of the Edwardian period Bangor was the premier seaside resort in Northern Ireland, attracting both day trippers and holidaymakers. All along the seafront hotels, cafés, restaurants and cinemas catered for visitors and the town's popularity continued through the inter-war years, right into the 1960s. But after that the introduction of foreign package holidays led to a serious decline in the number of holidaymakers, a decline which was exacerbated by the 'Troubles' in the 1970s, during which Bangor suffered from four car-bombs. However, today Bangor is enjoying something of a revival in tourism and, with the expansion of an excellent marina and associated activities, it is attracting visitors once more.

The wide expanse of the Esplanade is seen in this view of the junction of Bridge Street and Quay Street with Ballymagee Street (now known as High Street). Touring charabancs are lined up at the kerb, while their passengers enjoy the various treats on offer at the seaside. Some are enjoying a drink at the fountain under the Coates Memorial. According to its plaque, this was 'erected by the Members of the Bangor Corinthian Sailing Club in memory of their true friend Mrs Arthur Hill Coates 1893'. The husband of Mrs Coates was the Royal Ulster Yacht Club's Honorary Secretary from 1870 to 1880. The Bangor Corinthian Sailing Club was formed in 1880.

A view from the Esplanade, looking towards Quay Street. Shown here in its original position on the Esplanade, the bandstand was moved to the Marine Gardens when the McKee Clock was built in 1915. Quay Street had many fine buildings in it. The first tall building on the left is the Windsor Hotel and next to it is the turreted Grand Hotel. The next building was the Belfast Bank, built in 1866, which is now the Petty Sessions Court. Next to it is the Victoria Restaurant which was built in 1860. Pim's Stores, owned by E. and W. Pim, was a grocery emporium which specialised in tea. Founded around 1840, they were also wine merchants. Next door is Peveril House Hotel, while the rounded building on the corner with Ballymagee Street was erected in 1860.

This postcard was posted in 1943. The Sunken Gardens replaced the Esplanade in the 1930s (with later alterations occurring in the 1950s), and the area retained this appearance well into the latter part of the last century when it became part of the Marina development. The McKee Clock was built in 1915 and named after James McKee, the Borough Rates Collector, who offered the local council £200 to erect it. In this view there is plenty of commercial activity going on – a horse-drawn bread van belonging to the Inglis Bakery of Belfast is making its way into Queen's Parade, while two vendors sell 'frozen joy' from their tricycles. In the background, to the left of the clock, can be seen the Harbour Master's house which was built around 1860. It had a basement which was used as a boat house leading to a slipway. By the time of this photograph, two new hotels had been built to the left of the Royal Hotel.

An early view of Bridge Street with the cattle fair in progress. The buildings along Queen Street had not yet been developed into hotels. A market at Bangor was first established in 1605 and the weekly market is still very much a feature of life in Bangor.

At low tide the sandy beach between the piers was very popular with children. It was close to the hotels and the area was known as Children's Corner. There were donkey rides and many sandcastle competitions.

Pierrots were clowns or comic singers who usually performed at seaside resorts. In this photograph they are performing on the bandstand in the gardens in front of the Esplanade Hotel at the bottom of Ballymagee Street. The Pierrots in Bangor were most closely associated with the Regent Palace Hotel on Queen's Parade, where they would have entertained when the weather was inclement. To the left of the picture is the Jubilee Café, and on its right the Visitor's Café. Through the bandstand can be seen Bridge House, at one time the home of a Dr Higginson, which was converted to shops around 1910.

This card was posted to Pittsburg, Pennsylvania, in 1932. The spire of the First Bangor Presbyterian Church dominates the skyline, while Bridge Street and the intersection of Main Street and Queen's Parade contain many buildings to provide for holidaymakers and day trippers. The Criterion Hotel is the first building on the left, while next to it is the Jubilee Café, with its Dutch gable upon which stand the statues of two children. Next were the Boulevard and the Visitor's cafés, side by side with their striped slated roofs. The buildings on the right hand corner of Main Street are interesting in their contrasting uses. The building with the Dutch gable end is the Wesley Hall which is connected at the rear to the Queen's Parade Methodist Church. The church was built in 1891 to replace an earlier Methodist meeting house which had been on the site from 1821. On the front of the Methodist Hall is a sign which reads 'No drunkard will inherit the Kingdom of God', but despite this on the corner stands John Lynch's Central Bar. Most of these buildings remain, whereas many of those in the upper part of Main Street were destroyed by bombings during the 'Troubles'.

This view of Main Street, looking down towards Bangor Bay, was printed on a postcard posted in 1920. On the left is the Imperial Hotel which was owned in 1905 by W.H. Miller. By the 1930s it was known as 'The Widow's' as its owner by then was Widow Morgan. Sergeant Buchanan, the last Town Sergeant of Bangor, lived in the house next door and this later became Mawhinney's butcher's shop which is still in business today. Further down on the left, just before the entrance to King Street, is Scrabo House which was built around 1890 and was at one time a lending library. On the right hand side is the Downshire Restaurant and Temperance Hotel which in 1910 advertised that it could seat two hundred people comfortably. Two doors down is the shop of Sam Nelson the ironmonger (see page 37).

This postcard of Main Street was posted in 1907 by a young boy to his home in Paisley, Scotland. He wrote that 'the weather here is rotten. I am beginning to wish I was home, Jimmie.' At a time before cars were common, this photograph was taken from a point across the road from First Bangor Presbyterian Church (the railings of which are on the right) and looking towards the spire of Bangor Abbey. The castle (a house built in 1852) and demesne wall may be seen opposite the station. One of the houses on the right, beside the church grounds, was the manse.

Appearing on a postcard sent in 1935, this photograph of Queen's Parade was taken from the end of Southwell Road. Formerly known as Sandy Row, Queen's Parade was named after Queen Alexandra, who visited the town in 1903 with her husband, King Edward VII, and was driven along the sea front. The octagonal corner turret of the Strand Hotel still stands, although the premises are now occupied by McBurney's bar. In the background, on the right, the gasworks chimney can be seen. The works were demolished in 1988.

This photograph, printed on a postcard sent from Primrose Cottage in 1911, is of Dufferin Avenue, viewed from Bryansburn Road and looking towards Main Street and the railway station. The avenue was named after the First Marquis of Dufferin and Ava. Primrose Cottage was built about 1880 on a site between Dufferin Avenue and Princetown Road, but was demolished as part of a road widening scheme in 1935. Its site is now taken by a roundabout, although the name plaque from the cottage found its way to No. 39 Ballyholme Esplanade, pictured on page 21. On the left the neat West End Terrace, built around 1890, is still standing, although like many others its railings were removed for the manufacture of armaments during the Second World War. The West End Stores on the corner of Southwell Road is still in business.

Ballymagee Street became High Street in the early 1900s when it was thought that the town required another street with a commercial sounding name. Viewed from its intersection with Bridge Street and Quay Street, all the buildings date from around 1890 and most are still in place. Among other items, J. Camlin and Co. (on the left) sold 'celebrated Shamrock Unshrinkable Underclothing' This building was originally the Dufferin Restaurant Hotel, Dining and Billiard Rooms. Next to it is Captain Montgomery's Ulster Arms which offered dinners, lunches and teas. T. Marsh owned the next shop along, and next door to it is the attractive building of the Empire Hotel. The Alexandra Hotel is the first building on the right, while next door is the Central Fish Hall – the large gold fish hung outside it until it was blown down in a gale. This shop is still run by the McKeown family. Shanks was a public house. The horse drawn bread van advertising 'first class medal bread' belonged to McWatter's Bakery, Belfast.

A view looking down Ballymagee Street towards the bandstand and Bangor Bay. Most of these buildings remain intact. The fine buildings on Princetown Road can be seen across the bay. A charabanc belonging to the Reliance Motor Service, which began in 1908 and ran between Bangor and Donaghadee, is crowded with people making their way to the sea front. This postcard was sent from an army camp, possibly at Clandeboye; the message reads: 'the charabancs take us here from the camp, an hour's walk, for the marvellously cheap rate of 2/-. I usually go to a tea shop at the far end, after walking down. They have fine teas for a bob, and I prefer to waste my money in that direction.'

These three people are crossing Princetown Road, probably to make their way to the seafront by way of Tennyson Avenue, around 1912. The road was developed in the 1880s and '90s. The grand terrace on the right is Mayfield, which stand in some contrast to the modest Ardmore cottages on the opposite side of the road.

A view from Queen's Parade looking up Gray's Hill. The first large house on the parade, with the flagpole and yardarm, housed Abernethy's Studio. The proprietor, William Abernethy, specialised in studio portraits.

This postcard, sent in 1912, shows Windmill Hill which was in existence as a thoroughfare as early as 1830 and is now called Sheridan Drive. The post office building is still in place with its flat roof, although it now houses the shop Heritage and Heraldry. The two houses further down on the right were built in 1910 for one family. After the first was built they realised that it was too small, so they built an identical house next door. The site of the barn on the left was taken by Ballyholme Roman Catholic Church in 1931.

Ballyholme Bay is to the east of Bangor Bay and was developed later than the part of town closer to the railway station. The bay had the best beach in the area and was another popular bathing place in Bangor. In 1914 the council erected thirty bathing boxes; these were removed in the late 1960s, by which time they were rarely used and had become a target for vandalism.

Ballyholme Esplanade runs parallel to the beach above a grassy slope. Nearest on the right is Victoria Terrace, built in 1890. No. 39 has the name plaque from Primrose Cottage. The junction with Sheridan Drive is between this and the next terrace, Bay View Terrace. The front of Bayview House is in the background on the left, looking on to the open fields which have since been developed.

At one time this was the only pier at Bangor. A wall down the centre separates the working area on the left, where cargo handling was carried out, from where the Belfast passenger service berthed on the right. On the left is a small coasting vessel which had probably bought coal from the west of Scotland. Two new piers were later added at either side of this one. The harbour's position never afforded it a great deal of shelter and as a result development was restricted. The wooden section at the end was replaced by concrete in 1932. This pier now provides shelter for the very successful Bangor Marina.

The New Pier was built in 1896 at a cost of £24,000. The first 420 feet were concrete and beyond the turn there was 500 feet of open form pitch pine, which had been imported from Pensacola in Florida. It was furnished with a bandstand and in this view passengers are seen making their way ashore from the Belfast boat, while a small steam boat is leaving the steps, probably bound for the warships further out in the bay. It was not uncommon for several naval ships at a time to make courtesy visits to Bangor Bay.

This postcard, sent in 1908, shows the New Pier viewed from the Pickie Rock. The Belfast boat is just arriving, her decks crammed with day trippers. The vessel was owned by the Belfast and County Down Railway who operated the service after Moore Brothers went out of business in 1894. Later, regular timetabled services were replaced with excursions, the 'Bangor Boat' operating until 1939. After the Second World War the car became the prime mode of transport. The stone changing rooms in the foreground, on Pickie Rock, were erected in 1887 for the use of male bathers only – mixed bathing was not permitted until 1916. They were incorporated into the building of Pickie Pool in 1931.

The paddle steamer *Slieve Bearnagh* arriving at the New Pier sometime before 1912. This photograph gives a good idea of the size of the paddles at each side of the boat, and how useful they were in adding extra deck space for the fifty-five minute trip from Belfast. Operated by the Belfast and County Down Railway, she took over the service in 1894. The bollard on the quay is still in place today and is marked 'H. and J. Martin, Belfast, 1895'. The quay had upper and lower levels so that it could be used by disembarking passengers at both high and low tide.

The Belfast to Bangor steamer arriving in Bangor Bay in 1915. *Erin's Isle* replaced *Slieve Bearnagh* in 1912, but due to the interruption of the First World War the service was abandoned in 1915; the service resumed in 1918 and ran until 1939. Because the vessel was operated by the Belfast and County Down Railway, it was possible to purchase combined ship/rail tickets – many passengers liked to arrive by boat and return by train, or vice versa.

The 'Big Hole' (sometimes referred to as the 'Long Hole') is a small fjord-like inlet which provides shelter for fishing boats and other small craft. It is said that it is not natural, but was created when rock was quarried either for the building of a pier or the wall around the Castle demesne. Adjacent to the end of the New Pier, it runs along part of Seacliffe Road, on the right, which continues around Bangor Bay to Luke's Point. The road itself was just a track before becoming a proper thoroughfare in 1860. Since this photograph was taken, very little change has taken place to the terraces of houses along its length.

A view from the New Pier showing the Old Tower on Quay Street. This building has links back to the foundation of the town by Sir James Hamilton as it was built as the harbour's Custom House when he was granted a warrant to make Bangor a maritime port in 1620. It is still in use today as a tourist information office. To the left of the picture are the Adelaide Tearooms and the Harbour Café and, next along, the terrace in Victoria Road is the Tower Buildings, built by Charles Neill in 1890. At the top of the slipway is the Harbour Master's house which was built around 1860, the lower part being the boathouse. Until recently it was used by the lifeboat, but this is no longer possible as the area of sea in front of the slipway was filled in to make an area for the storage of yachts. This building is now a restaurant.

The message on the back of this postcard, sent in 1912, described this area, where Queen's Parade meets Somerset Avenue, as 'a very pretty place'. The gardens in the foreground belong to Nos. 61 and 62 Queen's Parade, a house called Emmavale. While the railings have been removed, the urns and gate pillars remain. The steps on the left lead up to Mount Pleasant and the large houses beyond are on Princetown Road. The building with the large bay windows at the side is 'Augustaville' which was built in 1887. On the seafront Lenaghan's rowing boats are stacked, ready for hire and awaiting the high tide.

The Pickie Rock was the site where, in the mid-1800s, swimming races were started. Development of a pool began when a Mr McFall of the Royal Hotel erected bathing boxes on the rock, and in 1919 the Bangor Amateur Swimming Club was formed and they swam at the rock. By the time of this photograph, Pickie Pool had been extended and the 'Great Opening' was held on Saturday, 30 May 1931. The diving board was 35 feet high and the pool 100 feet square. The pool was demolished in 1991 and is now the site of a fun park.

The Ladies' Bathing Place was just around the coast from the Pickie Rock. Following the provision of facilities for men, a local newspaper declared that 'we hope at least equal consideration will be shown to the fair visitors to Bangor, and that someone imitating Mr McFall's example will erect a suitable bathing-place for ladies'. Here is proof that some effort was made and parts of this pool are still visible today. The ladies in their swimming costumes appear to have attracted a gathering of men on the far shore – at one time there was a by-law which prohibited men from approaching any nearer than 100 yards! This photograph must have been taken from a boat and shows two large villas, Glenbank and Seacourt, on Princetown Road.

The Belfast and County Down Railway line to Bangor opened in May 1865. The station was designed by the Belfast firm of Lanyon, Lynn and Lanyon in the Italianate style and was composed of a large brick building with an imposing wooden façade and had a large concourse containing shops. The wall and trees around the castle and the demesne on the left were removed for road-widening in the 1960s.

IF YOU WANT TO GET THE BEST OUT OF BEAUTIFUL BANGOR

BEWARE of **BETTING** & **BOOZE**

On approaching Bangor Station
I observed with agitation
An arresting intimation
Published Large and Full and Free
To beware those sins besetting
Namely - Booze and likewise Betting,
Did they know that YOU were setting
For the Sea ?

There is a tradition in Ulster for farmers who wish to preach a certain message to the public to use the side of their red corrugated iron barns to promote it. This barn was part of Matthew's Yard, a firm of agricultural contractors on the outskirts of town. Visitors arriving in Bangor from Belfast by train were left in no doubt as to the potential evils that awaited them in the town. A similarly worded statement was on the rafters of Bangor Railway Station, but one wonders how many visitors heeded these words of advice!

The Northern Ireland Institute for the Disabled was founded as a Christian charity in 1878 and has been located in Bangor since 1898. Since the early 1900s it has been housed at the Stewart Memorial Home. This wonderful building was one of three similar type homes built on a small promontory overlooking Smelt Hill Bay. It was 'Erected to the glory of God and in loving memory of Lydia Montgomery Stewart who died 18th March 1900, wife of James Stewart, Beechmount, Donegall Park, Belfast'. The building has been extended on several occasions, most recently in 1992. The institute is currently undertaking a programme of housing development for the disabled around this building.

Trinity Presbyterian Church is situated in Main Street and was built in 1888. It is flanked on the left by the Main Street Pharmacy and on the right by the grocer A. Millsom.

As he had done in many towns, in the early 1900s Andrew Carnegie, the millionaire philanthropist, offered £1,500 for the building of a free library in Bangor, providing a site could be obtained. The Hon. Somerset Ward, Lord Clanmorris, gave the site on Hamilton Road, but Bangor Council wished to have the technical school in the building as well as the library. Carnegie was unhappy about this and reduced his offer to £1,250. However, the building went ahead and the Marquis of Londonderry opened the Carnegie Library and Municipal Technical School in January 1910. It remains the town's public library. Note the couple returning from a game of golf – at this time Bangor Golf Club was only a hundred yards or so down Hamilton Road.

The Regent Palace Hotel was situated in Queen's Parade and was built in 1931 at a cost of £20,000. Before it was demolished in the 1990s it was the Queen's Court Hotel.

Sam Nelson was listed in the trade directories of the early 1900s as an oil merchant and ironmonger. However, it is clear from this picture of his shop in Main Street that he stocked just about everything. The little dresser to the right appears to house Goss china crested souvenirs which were collected at the time by holidaymakers throughout the British Isles.

Below left: Viewed from what is now Church Street, Bangor Abbey was a monastic site as early as AD 555 when the monastery was established by Saint Comgall. It was razed by Viking raiders in the early ninth century. The restoration of the abbey was completed in 1126 by Saint Malachy. The English dissolved the monastery in 1542. The current abbey was built from the stones of its predecessor and the spire was added in 1693. Posted in 1902, the correspondent on this postcard wrote 'this is the church in which I was christened and went to Sunday School. Spire built in 1693, in good repair yet. Had a talk today with my S.S. teacher of 28 years ago. Pretty old.' With the increase in the size of the congregation, a larger church was required and Saint Comgall's Parish Church was opened in Hamilton Road in 1882. After this the abbey declined in importance, but in 1916, due to a further increase in the congregation's numbers, efforts were made to restore it and it was reopened in 1917. The Parish of Bangor Abbey was created in 1941.

Right: The windmill at Ballyholme gave its name to surrounding roads such as Windmill Hill and Windmill Lane. It dates from around 1780, but ceased to be a mill in 1922 following a fire. Nathaniel McCready was the last operator. Later, its upper part was removed just above the level of the third window on the right and it was given a castellated top. At one time the building was used by the Third Bangor Scout Troop, but it is now a private residence with cottages attached to the left-hand side.

The original Bangor Cottage Hospital stood in Hamilton Road and was established in 1869. It closed in 1910 when it was replaced by this building in Castle Street. At the time the setting was quite rural and overlooked Ward Park. A Miss Connor gave £500 towards the construction costs and the site was given rent-free by Lord and Lady Clanmorris. This building is easily recognisable today as part of Bangor Community Hospital and it now houses the Child Development Team. To the left is Castlemount Terrace which was built in 1895, and on the right is the glazed roof lantern on Hamilton Road Presbyterian Church.

Few yacht clubs in the world can have a more impressive club house overlooking their sailing waters than the Royal Ulster Yacht Club. Situated on Clifton Road, close to Ballyholme, in an area known as Garratt's Field, the club house was designed by Vincent Craig. A member of the club, he was a brother of Sir James Craig who later became Lord Craigavon. Builders McLaughlin and Harvey completed the building in sixteen months and the cost, including land and furnishings, was £8,157. Its official opening was on 15 April 1899 and it was reported that 300 ladies and gentlemen attended a reception. This was followed by an inaugural dinner for the sixty members and guests. A special train ran from Belfast for the event. This photograph shows the club house on Regatta Day shortly after its opening. It was as a member of this club that Sir Thomas Lipton made his five challenges for the America's Cup.

Ward Park, pictured around 1927. Bangor is fortunate to have two large green areas within its confines. Ward Park, the smaller of these, was the site of Bryce's brickworks and when these closed at the end of the nineteenth century the Ward family, who were landlords of the works, gave the area to the people of the town. The gardens were landscaped and a bowling green and two tennis courts were provided. The town's war memorial is in the park and the heavy gun in the picture was captured during the First World War. It was taken from the German submarine UB 19 and was presented to the town by the Admiralty in honour of Barry Bingham, commander of the destroyer *Nestor*, who won a Victoria Cross at the Battle of Jutland. Another Bangor landmark is the glazed roof lantern on Hamilton Road Presbyterian Church which was built in 1898. Although part of the original design, the vestibule and tower were only added in 1966!

A crowd of young people pictured below The Bungalow at Strickland's Glen, which runs down to Smelt Hill Bay just to the west of Bangor Bay. The Bungalow was built about 1915 to provide restaurant facilities in the glen, which had been purchased for public use in 1913. It had been demolished by 1940. The glen may have been named after a miller who operated in the vicinity in the late eighteenth century.

When King Edward VII and Queen Alexandra visited Bangor on 27 July 1903 this was the first visit to the town of a reigning monarch. The royal party arrived by sea and drove around the town in their coach before journeying on to Belfast by train. They are seen here at the Children's Stand which was erected for the occasion at Bridge Street.

The Merry Mascots, a group of entertainers who performed at Bangor in the early 1900s.

Henry Wingfield, pictured playing the three keyboard Compton organ with its illuminated rising console in Bangor's Tonic Cinema. As the music began the console rose out of the floor and with its changing colours was both a great sight and sound. The Tonic opened in July 1936 and could hold up to 2,000 people. It closed in 1983, but fortunately the organ was saved and is now in Gransha Boys' High School on Bangor's Gransha Road. The Tonic Cinema suffered a large fire in June 1992 and had to be demolished.

Groomsport is a village two miles east of Bangor. A harbour has existed there for hundreds of years and it was formerly known as Gilgroomesport, 'the port of the gloomy servant'. The harbour is reputed to be the landing place in 1689 of the Duke of Schomberg and an army of 10,000 men. He was an ally of William of Orange and they met the following summer on the way to the Boyne. A lifeboat house was built in 1884 and extensions to the pier were made around 1902. Previously the harbour would have served the local fishing fleet, but is used more now by leisure craft. There is a local sailing club, known as the Cockle Island Boat Club. While many of the small buildings in front of the church have been demolished, those to the left of the sail of the yacht have been preserved. This is Cockle Row, which is over three hundred years old.

This early view of Groomsport shows the type of housing, similar to that still standing in Cockle Row, which was present well into the twentieth century. In fact, it was not until the 1960s that the houses on the left – occupied by the Bell, Lindsay, Orr and Tosh families – were demolished to make space for a park. Groomsport Presbyterian Church is to the right, while on the left, at the bottom of the street, is the parish church. This was endowed by Waring Maxwell, a Tory MP for Downpatrick, and was built in 1842 to the design of Charles Lanyon, the famous Belfast architect.

Facing onto Bangor's Donaghadee Road, the Savoy Hotel – or to give it its full name, the New Savoy Hotel – is a very impressive Art Deco style building dating from 1932. It was built for Mr J. Gaston of Northern Ireland Tours and throughout its time as a hotel it was open for just the thirteen weeks of the summer season each year. It is currently used as sheltered housing by the Royal British Legion Housing Association.